SUMMARY of Jocko Willink and Leif Babin's EXTREME OWNERSHIP

How U.S. Navy SEALS Lead and Win

by SUMOREADS

Copyright © 2017 by SUMOREADS. All rights reserved. This book or parts thereof may not be reproduced in any form, stored in any retrieval system, or transmitted in any form by any means—electronic, mechanical, photocopy, recording, or otherwise—without prior written permission of the publisher, except as provided by United States of America copyright law. This is an unofficial summary and is not intended as a substitute or replacement for the original book.

TABLE OF CONTENTS

EXECUTIVE SUMMARY 5
Introduction 6

PART I: WINNING THE WAR WITHIN 7
Chapter 1: Extreme Ownership 7
Chapter 2: No Bad Teams, Only Bad Leaders 8
Chapter 3: Believe 8
Chapter 4: Check the Ego 10

PART II: THE LAWS OF COMBAT 11
Chapter 5: Cover and Move 11
Chapter 6: Simple 11
Chapter 7: Prioritise and Execute 13
Chapter 8: Decentralized Command 14

PART III SUSTAINING VICTORY 15
Chapter 9: Plan 15
Chapter 10: Leading Up and Down the Chain of Command 15
Chapter 11: Decisiveness amid Uncertainty 16
Chapter 12: Discipline Equals Freedom – The Dichotomy of Leadership 17

KEY TAKEAWAYS 19
Key Takeaway: Good leadership is not a talent, but a discipline. 19
Key Takeaway: Failure is expected in leadership, managing failure is what defines leaders 19
Key Takeaway: Extreme Ownership is winning, not losing 20
Key Takeaway: Navy SEALs exhibit a brotherhood refined over time by training and discipline 20

Key Takeaway: No team is bad, but leaders can be 21
Key Takeaway: Leaders are competitive but gracious losers.. 21
Key Takeaway: Leaders are confident but not cocky 21
Key Takeaway: The Battle of Ramadi was not about U.S. forces, but about Iraqis.. 22

EDITORIAL REVIEW 23

ABOUT THE AUTHORS 25

EXECUTIVE SUMMARY

In their book *Extreme Leadership: How U.S. Navy SEALS Lead and Win*, Jocko Willink and Leif Babin explore qualities of exceptional leadership using lessons learned in the military through their leadership in various positions in SEALs teams. The book documents lessons learned specifically in The Battle of Ramadi, Iraq in 2006.

In the book, Babin and Willink keenly replicate the battleground environment and outline the processes involved in staging a successful security operation. They show the tactical, logistical, collaborative and intellectual investment that the U.S. Navy SEALs constantly employ to lead and win, as well as the emotional pain they brave when they lose their own.

The authors use combat experiences and lessons from the SEAL involvement in the Battle of Ramadi to show how leadership skills are learned, harnessed, and employed in battle and, by extension, beyond military uses including business, negotiations, and personal growth and development. The book discusses major qualities of a good leader, among them the ability to manage ego, taking ownership of outcome, applying discipline, prioritizing and executing procedures in a logical manner, delegation, and becoming decisive during uncertainty.

The authors marry their military lessons with their consultancy advice for senior company officials looking to apply exceptional leadership skills to grow their businesses.

Introduction

The Combat Leader

This book is written as a dedication to SEAL officers who fought in the Battle of Ramadi, Iraq in the year 2006. It is not a self-praising work, but a reflection on the experiences of the various U.S and Iraqi security forces who bravely faced and prevailed against the brutal Sunni insurgent regime. It is a book about the Iraqi people and how the SEALS forces participated in restoring freedom to them. It explains in detail the day to day life of a soldier in general, and more specifically the SEAL team, in a constant battlefield. The authors courageously mourn fallen teammates while dedicatedly pursuing the call of duty and learning from their mistakes.

This book demonstrates how SEAL teams develop high-performance units and develop leadership skills to lead and win.

PART I: WINNING THE WAR WITHIN

Chapter 1: Extreme Ownership

Mal'aab District, Iraq

A ground force comprised of four SEAL teams, US Army Scout snipers, and Iraq Defense Forces is on a mission to clear a particularly hostile portion of this metropolis. Forces on the ground are heavily engaged and requesting a Quick Reaction Force (QRF). In the ensuing confusion, a SEAL sniper shoots a friendly officer from the Iraqi Defense Force (IDF). Back at the base, the author demonstrates extreme ownership during the situation briefing, probably saving his job, by taking full responsibility of the blue-on-blue (a confusion in which friendly fire is exchanged). The author avoids making excuses, though he justifiably may show that he was not culpable—there were other commanders in charge of the allied IDF.

The author applies this lesson to advise a company's vice president on how to manage faults. In his advice, the VP should learn to take the blame for all non-performing subsidiaries, divisions, and units in his company because he has failed to communicate to them effectively and make them own up to the greater goal—the company's success. In addition, he should not shy away from relieving non-performing personnel.

Chapter 2: No Bad Teams, Only Bad Leaders

Coronado, California

The author is a training supervisor in the intensive one-week Basic Underwater Demolition (BUD) SEAL training. This training (Hell Week) is intended to harden SEAL officers and enhance their endurance skills in real battle situations. They sleep less than one hour in three days and are made to carry Inflatable Boat Smalls (IBS) up and down the ocean line repeatedly in teams of six under soaking wet sea water conditions. The author observes how Team 2 always finished first, while Team 6 always trailed. When team leaders were swapped, Team 6 consistently came first while Team 2 consistently came second. This demonstrated the role of strong leadership in winning.

The author shares this experience with a top company official during a consultancy session in which the company official presents the "Tortured Genius Mentality" as a defense for poor leadership—effectively changing his outlook and leadership strategy.

Chapter 3: Believe

Jocko Willink, Shark Base: Camp Ramadi

The author has received orders from the security headquarters to include officers from the Iraqi Defense Forces in all the security operations. This new plan greatly jeopardizes the safety and efficiency of the SEAL teams and U.S. Army officers as the local military is not well trained enough to fight alongside them. Ground officers view this new plan as a sure death trap and reject it outright. The author realizes, after deep thought, that there are two reasons they should include the local military in their operations.

First, the IDF officers know the terrain and building access tricks better than U.S. forces. They also know the accents and mannerisms of suspicious persons when identifying hiding insurgents. Secondly, and more importantly, the local IDF will be expected to defend their country when the U.S. withdraws its troops. They must be prepared for this future through participation in present operations. For the author and commanding officer, these two perspectives of reasoning presented greater meaning in this problem than the safety of working alone would.

The immediate and hardest part is explaining this new perspective to the teams working under him in order for them to understand why working with the less qualified IDF is ultimately the best decision. A good leader always asks their superiors *why?*, and explains the same to their juniors.

"In order to convince and inspire others to follow and accomplish a mission, a leader must be a true believer in the mission" (p. 76).

The author uses this concept to explain to a company executive why their competitive sales compensation plan of rewarding top performers is not increasing sales for the company. The company needs to explain in detail *why* there appear to be inconsistencies in the way employees are getting their bonuses, as their complex formula is diminishing worker morale.

Chapter 4: Check the Ego

Jocko Willink, Camp Corregidor, Ramadi

Sunni insurgents have launched an overnight attack on a U.S. military outpost. The army and marine U.S. battalions are returning fire from their fortified rooftops using machine guns and round-up illuminators. Teams operating the M1A2 Abrams 120mm guns and the M2 Bradley Fighting Vehicles with 40mm explosive grenades join in the onslaught. An elite new Iraq fighting unit is brought in to join the 1/506th Battalion—a highly respected and traditionally disciplined army battalion. This Iraqi elite group, though highly qualified and matching the U.S. SEALs technical skills, exhibits a very egoistic outlook towards the joint assignment. Its officers refuse to report to anyone, fail to share coordination information, and rudely look down on other groups.

The commanding officer in the 1/506th battalion, in consultation with the author, exercises his discretion to terminate cooperation with the group, making it redundant despite their high qualifications. The author parallels this story of egoism to an issue with a drilling superintendent. Back in the business world, Willink advises a company official on how to handle a drilling superintendent whose high-headedness in decision making greatly costs the company. The author brings to the attention of the supervisor the reason behind their long-standing feud with the drilling superintendent (DS): himself. The supervisor's ego elicits a negative reaction in the DS. The supervisor should own up to the problem and elicit feelings of responsibility, not revenge or egoistic competition, in the DS.

PART II: THE LAWS OF COMBAT

Chapter 5: Cover and Move

South Central Ramadi, Iraq

All U.S. forces including Team Bulldog (Bravo Company, 1st Battalion, 37th Armored Regiment), SEAL team from Charlie Platoon, and SEALs from Task Unit Bruiser are in an operation in a highly volatile region of Ramadi. SEALS provide sniper overwatch while combat advisors from the U.S. Army manage ground troops. After a successful operation, the author pulls his troops back to combat outpost (COP) without incorporating cover from other units in the area. The mission commander takes offense at the author for failing to utilize available cover, thereby jeopardizing his troops. Good leadership is about incorporating teamwork.

The author uses this concept to broaden a company executive's perspective of teamwork in harnessing synergy—rather than competition and apathy—between subsidiaries of a large company. The senior official realizes that if one subsidiary fails, regardless of which it is, the whole company is affected.

Chapter 6: Simple

Combat Outpost Falcon, Ramadi

A night of overhead insurgent attacks on the COP leaves several soldiers wounded by mortar shells. The U.S Army officer in charge of IDF (MiTTS) shares with the author a plan to launch a deep insurgent territory offensive. The author conducts a brief situation analysis and concludes that the proposal is laden with serious security threats since the proposed area is deep in the enemy territory. The MiTTS team may be well beyond practical reinforcement range if ambushed, and the use of the M1A2 Abrams and Bradley vehicles may not be practical as that route is laden with IEDs. The author suggests that the MiTTS team starts simple, avoiding complex engagement that may jeopardize their operational efficiency. The author's advice proves useful as 12 minutes later the MiTTS team is attacked near building J51. The author arranges rapid backup—CASEVAC, fire support, and SEAL overwatch—and the MiTTS team is rescued.

The rescue mission relies on the use of simple and timely tactics and communication from the coordinating forces including SEAL teams, firepower teams, the U.S. Army, and the IDF. This chapter demonstrates the use of simple and concise plans and actions in winning a battle as a good leadership trait.

The author uses this concept to advise a company's representative on the importance of maintaining a simple rationale in calculating sales bonuses for its employees. He informs the executive that not understanding the rules upon which bonuses are gained effectively reduces employee motivation. The executive finally simplifies his approach to help the workers understand the bonus calculation concept.

Chapter 7: Prioritise and Execute

Leif Babin, South Central Hamadi, Iraq.

Another insurgent attack sends the author and SEAL troops to take cover on the COP rooftop. SEALs subdue and kill insurgents. The team plans a clearance operation in the night. They sneak onto a vantage from an abandoned three-story building from which they launch a successful day-long onslaught. As their explosive experts place charges to detonate IEDs placed in the exit point by insurgents, the SEAL team digs an exit hole on the building's side that leads them to the roof of an adjacent one-story building. A SEAL officer falls through the roof and needs emergency evacuation. In addition, the dawn is fast approaching, and with it an almost certain attack from the enemy. The team must prioritize their actions in order to realize a winning outcome.

"Relax, look around, make a call" (p.161).

The strategy applied by the author and his team demonstrate the importance of setting priorities as a leader and executing them in a logical order. To win in a confusing situation, a leader starts by determining the highest priority action, then they determine the most important move, devise a solid and simple strategy, and finally execute. The author applies this approach to assist a company executive torn between promoting different aspects of company expansion. The author helps the chief executive to prioritize one department of sales, and concentrate on it fully.

Chapter 8: Decentralized Command

Jocko Wilink, South Central Ramadi, Iraq

A SEAL officer attached to the author's platoon has spotted a sniper with a weapon several blocks across the street and is hesitant about taking him out. He consults the author, who, having extensive experience and training including the Military Operation Urban Terrain (MOUT), and with the understanding that there could unexpectedly be friendly forces on that rooftop, decides to consult other team leaders. He gets clearance that the sniper is not a friendly troop and is advised to engage, but relies on instinctive doubt to hold longer. Later, the author realizes that the sniper is friendly, that his team had mistaken the house number. The author realizes the need for a decentralizing channel of command allowing people working under him to make decisions. Good leadership is about empowering people in lower ranks to take initiative and understand the best course of action towards success.

The author uses this lesson in advice to a company president who has field managers directly in charge of more than 20 personnel. He advises the manager that to have greater success, he should fragment field forces in groups of 4–6, and delegate some authority to their leaders.

PART III: SUSTAINING VICTORY

Chapter 9: Plan

Ramadi, Iraq

An Iraqi colonel's son is held hostage by Sunni insurgents for $50,000 in the outskirts of Ramadi. The threat is real, and the author knows the location is likely to be wired with IEDs and under sentries with machine guns. Rescuing the hostage will require a meticulously fine-tuned plan. The SEAL special team manages to rescue the hostage without casualties. The author holds that to succeed in emergency operations such as the rescue, the plan needs to have three aspects: the element of surprise, speed, and positive identification of the target.

The author demonstrates the use of discipline in leadership during a consultancy with a company president. He advises the president to create a repeatable process of creating new markets to avoid resource waste and ambiguity.

Chapter 10: Leading Up and Down the Chain of Command

Camp Mac Lee, Ramadi

The author recounts how U.S. security positions inside Ramadi came under attack or initiated clearance operations themselves, and how they managed to succeed in suppressing the insurgency. Later, in the U.S. while briefing the Chief of Naval Operations on the details of the mission of Ramadi, he is surprised by the precision and detail needed by the chief in filling out the information.

The author is surprised at the complexity of the interplay of the activities of the various security forces including SEAL teams, U.S Navy and Army forces, and the Iraqi Defense Forces, that was needed to simply coordinate the Battle for Ramadi. At this point, he realizes how difficult contemplating and comprehending the point by point activities in the mission was, on top of understand how they were all connected. This leads him to understand how much their coordination contributed to the mission's success.

Only at this moment does the author appreciate how confusing the activities in the entire mission might have been for the teams. He feels a deep sense of liability and extreme ownership for failing to sufficiently inform his juniors of the exact ways in which all activities conducted during the mission were interconnected in achieving the final goal.

Good leadership is about exercising leadership upwards and downwards. A leader briefs his superiors and juniors sufficiently and ensures everyone understands what is needed, and why every action is relevant.

Chapter 11: Decisiveness amid Uncertainty

Sniper Overwatch, Ramadi

Chris Kyle, a talented sniper and a leader in threat elimination attached to the author's SEALs team, spots a sniper whom he suspects to be an enemy but for some reason hesitates to eliminate him. On consultation, the sniper is found to be from a friendly team. Trusting his gut feeling, the author dissuades the sniper from taking the shot at the suspect, despite advice to act from other team leaders.

This concept is used by the author in advising the CEO of a software company whose two senior development officers have a long-standing feud and are both backbiting each other and threatening to leave the company. The CEO cannot imagine losing either, and even worse, losing other loyalists who might decamp with their leaders. The author advises the CEO to fire both senior officers in order to avoid an imminent crisis and promote other able officers to fill the positions.

Chapter12: Discipline Equals Freedom – The Dichotomy of Leadership

Jocko Willink, Baghdad, Iraq

The author relates the procedure that SEAL teams, with minimal evidence collection skills, employ to collect evidence to prosecute insurgents during home raids in Baghdad. SEALs typically break into homes and tear apart everything in sight to look for information or items that could possibly incriminate the homeowners, often emptying drawers and mixing up everything on the floor. This process is inefficient as often they end up missing critical areas, or repeating searches and wasting time.

The author instructs a deputy to design a prototype of methodical searching. The method categorically assigns every officer a particular area, avoiding duplication. It requires searches to follow a particular order, and for evidence to be clearly marked and uniquely attached to the original source house, and for all evidence to be methodically kept. This operational discipline greatly enhances the evidence assignment for the SEALs. Leaders are disciplined and methodical. They avoid ambiguity and spontaneity in the way they operate. They organize information logically and are therefore able to make accurate judgments easily.

"Every leader must walk a fine line" (p. 274).

The author uses this concept in advising a company owner to close down its electrical division which is headed by a close friend of the company owner, but generating losses. The author advises the company owner that good leadership is about mission discipline and that if the company is to stand, he must be disciplined in making difficult decisions with the end goal being the success of the business.

KEY TAKEAWAYS

Key Takeaway: Good leadership is not a talent, but a discipline.

The leadership traits described in most of the chapters including managing your ego; executing processes in a simple, logical order; and prioritizing your activities or actions are all elements of discipline. In contrast, exceptional leaders have been imagined as visionary or intelligent—qualities this book does not hold in esteem.

Key Takeaway: Failure is expected in leadership, managing failure is what defines leaders

The book defines at least half a dozen instances of extreme failures. Some lead to the deaths of troops, others critical mistakes that almost led to death, and still more that endangered entire teams or constituted serious protocol breaches. It is through these mistakes that true leadership qualities are tested, and good leaders identified. The author demonstrates qualities of essential leadership in managing failures or containing tension in his subordinates, which promotes the cohesiveness of the group and helps the SEAL teams and other units develop a winning synergy.

Key Takeaway: Extreme Ownership is winning, not losing

As a leader, extreme ownership means accepting all the shortcomings of the people working under you as your own. This outlook may seem as though it weakens your performance and positions you vulnerably with regard to career growth. In reality, this outlook demonstrates your commitment to the success of both yourself and your team. It motivates your subordinates to take responsibility and emulate your leadership style. This outlook also encourages leadership by example, because a leader who is willing to accept the mistakes of others is likely to set a good example as someone whose performance can be counted on.

Key Takeaway: Navy SEALs exhibit a brotherhood refined over time by training and discipline

The decorated and much respected U.S. Navy SEAL teams have evolved through several decades of experimental and strategic development phases. They endure extremely rigorous procedures to develop the SEAL profile—a highly disciplined and integrated profile geared towards teamwork in achieving dangerous work missions. They are a closed unit based on trust, where every member is the other member's strength and eyes. Because the nature of most of their assignments is one of extreme risk, they must equally rely on a bond that is of extreme trust.

Key Takeaway: No team is bad, but leaders can be

Teams tend to draw from their leader's energy. Weak leaders often make weak and fragmented teams that fail to achieve missions. Strong leaders tend to grow their teams to emulate themselves. They develop a synergy with their leader that reflects the intrinsic qualities the leader shows.

Key Takeaway: Leaders are competitive but gracious losers

Your leadership qualities show in winning as well as in losing. Accepting loss in a graceful way prepares you for the next battle, but grappling negatively with loss weakens your fighting spirit.

Key Takeaway: Leaders are confident but not cocky

Good leadership is about exhibiting confidence in making rational and timely decisions. It is not a show of might. It is about inclusiveness and consultation in decision making. Leadership reflects your internal wealth of self-esteem, calmness in difficult situations, resolve in executing your convictions, humility when under criticism, and bravery in safeguarding your team and your mission's interest. These traits elicit admiration, not scorn, from your juniors and approval from your superiors.

Key Takeaway: The Battle of Ramadi was not about U.S. forces, but about Iraqis

The battle of Ramadi, like every other battle that involved SEAL teams, was not about the U.S forces or their show of prowess and might. Battles in which SEAL teams fight are about a greater mission. In the Ramadi case, the battle was about restoring Ramadi from insurgents. The SEAL teams secretly took pride in their victory, but the official victory was for the Iraqi people who would not live in oppression under the illegitimate and brutal regime. Ultimately, leadership is not about personal glory, but about achieving a bigger goal. It is about changing people's lives.

EDITORIAL REVIEW

In their book *Extreme Leadership*, Jocko Willink and Leif Babin explore qualities of exceptional leadership using lessons learned in the military, specifically the Battle of Ramadi, Iraq in 2006.

In their book, Babin and Willink demonstrate the application of principles of leadership in battleground situations, especially in South Central Ramadi, to secure success. In *Extreme Ownership*, the authors hold that a good leader must accept responsibility for the actions of their juniors, regardless of how directly in control of these actions the leader is. In addition, the authors highlight other important attributes of good leadership including the ability to plan, to break down problems and execute them in a simple, logical priority-based manner, the ability to decentralize command through delegation and to make rational decisions even amid uncertainty.

The authors also warn against the ego, as it obscures one's ability to see a problem from all perspectives. They emphasize the importance of discipline in good leadership and regard having faith in your subordinates as a proper way to empower them and motivate them towards realizing the greater mission.

The book is well written, using practical field scenarios to validate all arguments. It is clearly and concisely authored, and avoids overuse of military jargon that may confuse leaders, but without compromising on vital information. The cause/effect logic is well cultivated, and the reader is carefully and exhaustively guided through the problem and logic of the solution. This work is an essential contribution to the field of modern leadership and more specifically, the effectiveness of the path-goal theory of leadership.

ABOUT THE AUTHORS

Jocko Willink and Leif Babin are former Navy SEAL officers who led the Task Unit Bruiser through the Battle of Ramadi in the year 2006. They built one of the most cohesive and successful SEAL teams through good leadership. They also have designed SEAL training programs for current and future groups back in the U.S.

The two leaders also pioneered Echelon Front, a leadership consultancy firm that specializes in knowledge support for companies and corporations looking to achieve good leadership skills.

THE END

If you enjoyed this summary, please leave an honest review on Amazon.com…it'd mean a lot to us.

If you haven't already, we encourage you to purchase a copy of the original book.

Made in the USA
San Bernardino, CA
16 January 2018